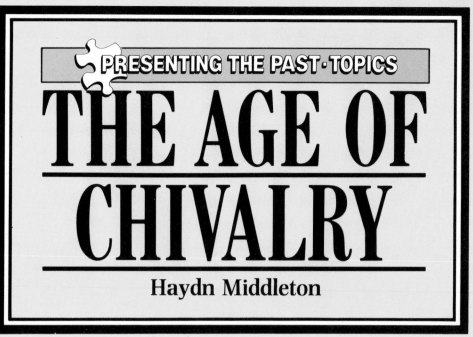

### PRESENTING THE PAST · TOPICS

# THE AGE OF CHIVALRY

#### Haydn Middleton

## Oxford University Press 1988

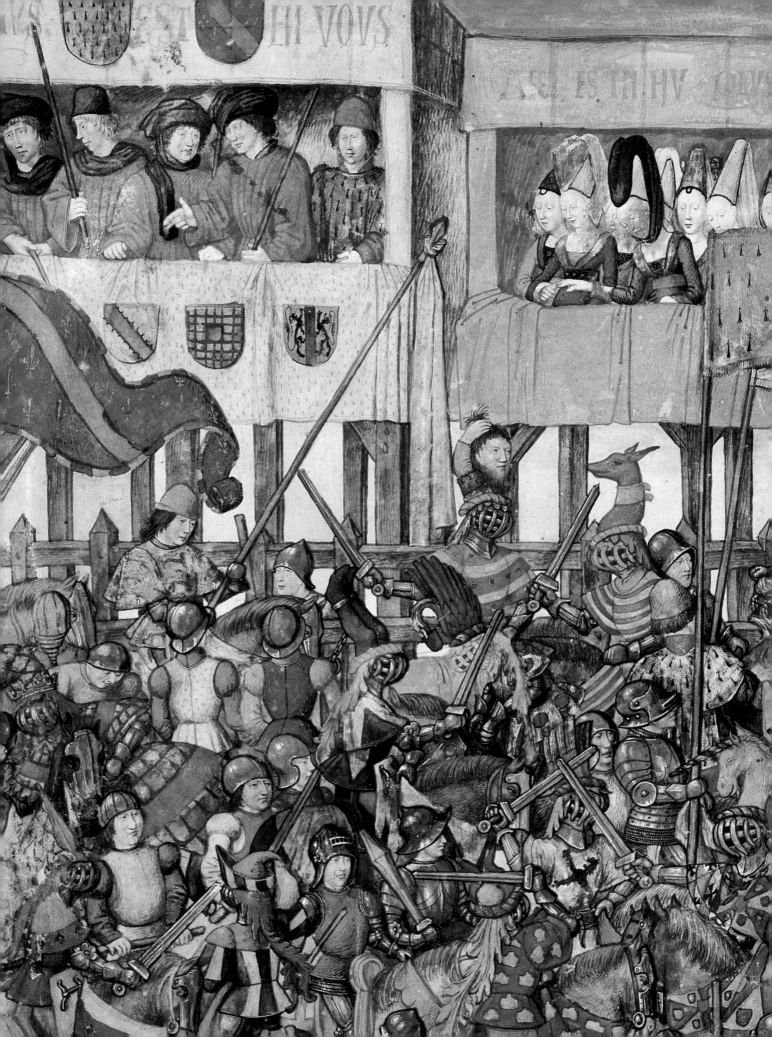

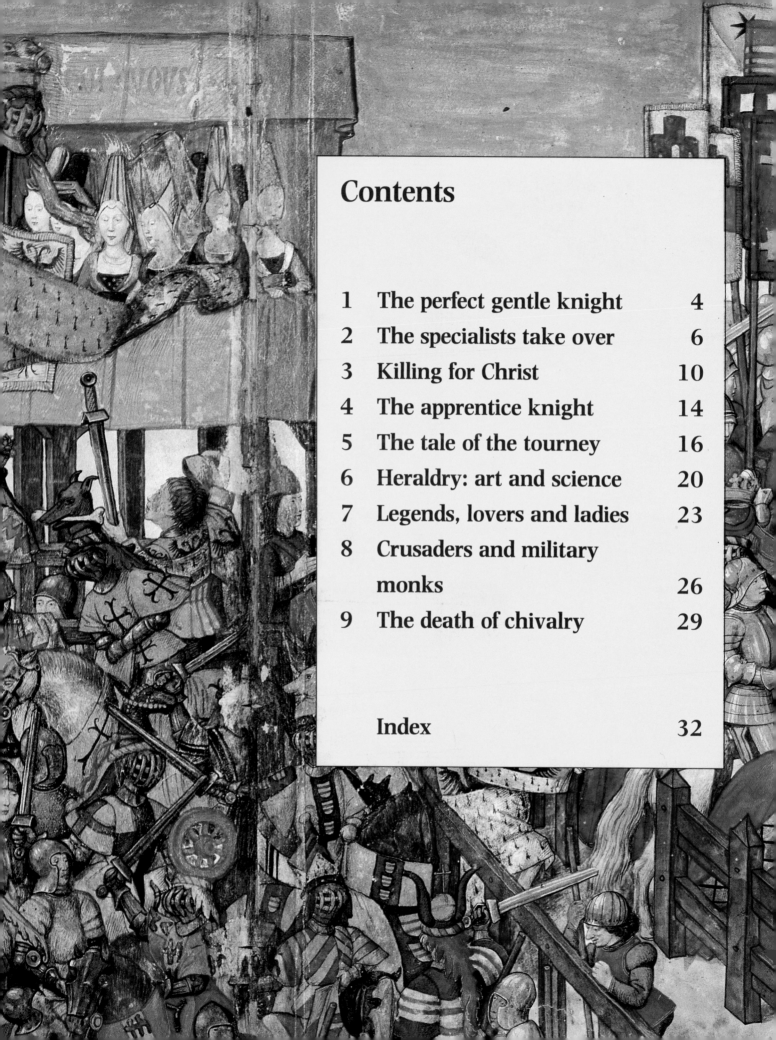

# Contents

# 1 The perfect gentle knight

The man on the right is a knight. Knights were medieval warriors. They were trained to fight on horseback with lances. You probably knew those things already. But what sort of men were knights? Were they young or old? How did they become knights in the first place? What did they do when they weren't fighting? And what did other people think of them?

There are some answers to these questions in this book. Often the information will come straight from the Middle Ages – from medieval writings and from medieval pictures. That picture on the right, for example, comes from a Norwegian tapestry made in the twelfth century. These 'sources' of information will help you to travel back in time to the world of the knights. And a very strange world it was too . . .

## An ideal knight

Soon you will be meeting some real medieval knights. But first, let's see how knights were supposed to behave if they were *absolutely* ideal. You see, an ideal knight had to be much more than a good warrior. The first description comes from a French poem, written in the twelfth century:

> 66 Lords, look at the best knight that you have ever seen. He is brave and courtly and skilful, and noble and of good family and eloquent, handsomely experienced in hunting and falconry; he knows how to play chess and backgammon, gaming and dicing. And his wealth was never denied to any, but each has as much as he wants . . . And he has never been slow to perform honourable deeds. He dearly loves God and the Trinity . . . And he always loved a good knight; he has honoured the poor and lowly; and he judges each according to his worth. 99
>
> *(Girart)*

Two hundred years later, another French poet gave this advice to those who longed to become knights:

> 66 You should lead a new life:
> Devoutly keeping watch in prayer,
> Fleeing from sin, pride and villainy;

> The Church defending,
> The widow and orphan helping,
> Be bold and protect the people,
> Be loyal and valiant, taking nothing from others.
> Thus should a knight rule himself.
>
> He should be humble of heart and always work
> And follow deeds of Chivalry;
> He should attend tourneys and joust for his lady love;
> He must keep honour with all
> So that he cannot be held to blame.
> No cowardice should be found in his doings,
> Above all he should uphold the weak,
> Thus should a knight rule himself. 99
>
> *(Eustace Deschamps)*

A knight like this had to be backed up by a large team. He needed at least one warhorse, a groom, an esquire (see page 14), perhaps a scout to spy out the land, even a couple of footsoldiers to stand guard. The whole team was called a 'lance'. It was 'like the crew of some enormous battle tank' writes Michael Howard, a modern historian.

4

## Following the code of chivalry

The second description on page 4 included the word 'chivalry'. So does the following one. It comes from an English book written in about 1380:

> 66There was a Knight, a most distin-
> guished man,
> Who from the day on which he first
> began
> To ride abroad had followed chivalry,
> Truth, honour, generousness and
> courtesy.
> He had done nobly in his sovereign's
> war
> And ridden into battle, no man more,
> As well in christian as in heathen
> places,
> And ever honoured for his noble
> graces.99 *(Geoffrey Chaucer)*

Chaucer called this character in his story 'a perfect gentle knight'. But what *was* this 'chivalry' that he followed? The word comes from 'chevalier', which is the French for 'knight'. In the descriptions above, 'chivalry' simply means: the aims and ideal behaviour of a true knight.

Medieval writers, who were mostly clergymen, tried to describe a 'code of chivalry'. This was a set of rules, to guide the thoughts and actions of knights. The caption (right) shows what qualities a 'chivalrous' knight should have. But there was never a single code which all the knights of Europe *had* to obey. And some knights actually ignored chivalrous ideals altogether. Why, then, did writers bother to describe chivalry so carefully? Why did they think that the knights *needed* a code to keep to? To answer those questions, we have to begin at the beginning. We have to go right back to the first knights of history . . .□

1 Describe, in your own words, how an *absolutely ideal* medieval knight should behave. Explain which qualities he should show above all others, and say *why* he should show them.

2 What were the three 'estates' of the Middle Ages? Do people belong to such estates nowadays? List any (i) good points (ii) bad points about thinking that people should belong to estates.

The **clergyman** (*far left*) prayed and kept everyone on the right side of God. The **labourer** (*left*) worked the land and provided the basic things of life. The warriors or knights lived in greater luxury than the labourers. But they were expected to behave well, and to set a good example. A truly chivalrous knight was meant to show: *prowess* (bravery, strength and skill), *loyalty, largesse* (generosity) and *courtesy* (kindness, politeness).

# 2 The specialists take over

Until the late 300s AD, western Europe belonged to the Roman Empire. (Britain was just one province of that Empire.) Throughout all the provinces, Roman soldiers kept the peace, and Christianity came to be the 'official' religion. Then things went terribly wrong. Pagan tribesmen broke into the Empire and swept across it, burning, raiding, spreading havoc wherever they went. The Romans could not deal with these sudden, repeated attacks on all sides. By the mid-400s the pagan 'barbarians' were in control of western Europe.

## Into the Dark Ages

The centuries after the break-up of the Roman Empire are called the Dark Ages. This is not just because time were bad. In some places, like Ireland, they were actually quite good! But our *picture* of those times is dark and unclear. This is partly because there were fewer writers then than there had been in Roman days – so we have less information about those times. But we do know that the barbarian tribesmen set up kingdoms and empires of their own. In England, for example, Anglo-Saxon invaders set up seven separate kingdoms. Meanwhile the headquarters of the Christian religion continued to be in Rome. And missionaries from Rome gradually converted the new pagan rulers of Europe to Christianity.

In Rome, on Christmas Day 800, the ruler of a people called the Franks was crowned Emperor. His name was Charlemagne. His Empire stretched from France in the west, across to central Europe, and down into Italy. He was a Christian. He was also the mightiest ruler in western Europe since the end of the Roman Empire. To remind people of these two facts, he called himself 'Holy Roman Emperor'. But just like the Roman Emperors of old, Charlemagne and his neighbours had to face fearsome invaders (see map). The question

Map legend:
- VIKINGS
- Area of the Christian West on eve of invasions
- Boundary of the Frankish Empire 814 AD
- 0    400    800 km
- Atlantic Ocean
- FRANKISH EMPIRE
- MAGYARS
- Mediterranean Sea
- SARACENS

*Above:* In the 9th and 10th centuries, Christian Europe was invaded from all sides. In the end the Magyars and Saracens were driven out. Many Vikings settled down and became Christians themselves, even in England.

*Right:* This picture, from a 9th-century psalm books, shows Charlemagne's cavalrymen and footsoldiers. The Franks relied more and more on cavalrymen in their armies. Notice how they are dressed in long surcoats of iron chainmail and not 'shining armour'!

6

was: how could they possibly drive these new barbarians back?

You see, Europe's rulers had no 'standing armies' to call on, no specially-trained forces. In times of emergency, all able-bodied men simply had to rally round their leader. Then they would fight, on foot, with whatever weapons they could lay their hands on – swords, spears, axes, even farm tools. These warriors fought bravely and loyally, but often that wasn't enough. The words below come from the English Anglo-Saxon Chronicle. ('The enemy' here were the Viking invaders.)

❝When the enemy was in the east, then our soldiers were gathered in the west; and when they were in the south, our soldiers were in the north. The king and his advisers had plans, but no one followed them for a single month. In the end, there was no leader who would get an army together, but each fled as quickly as he could.❞

The kings of England never really found a way of dealing with these Vikings. Soon after 1000, England became a part of the great Viking Empire. But over on the mainland of Europe, things were turning out rather differently . . .

## Mobile warriors

In 806 Charlemagne wrote this letter to one of his subjects, the Abbot of Altaich:

❝You shall come to the river Weser with your men prepared to go on warlike service to any part of our realm that we may point out: that is, you shall come with arms and gear and all warlike equipment of clothing and victuals [*supplies*]. Every horseman shall have shield, lance, sword, dagger, a bow and a quiver. On your carts you shall have ready spades, axes, picks, and iron-pointed stakes, and all other things needed for the host. The rations shall be for three months, the clothing must last for six.❞

This shows how well-organized Charlemagne wanted his armies to be. It also includes a key word – 'horsemen'. To deal with so many invaders, warriors had to get around fast. And when it came to fighting, mounted warriors – cavalrymen – had many advantages over foot-soldiers. So why hadn't anyone thought of using cavalrymen before? Well, they had.

There had been cavalrymen in the armies of the Roman Empire. Even the barbarian

This picture, from a book written in about 1028, shows some rough and ready warriors on horseback. You can imagine how fearsome they seemed to the people of the time. Men like these ate and drank like gluttons, to fuel themselves up for combat: 'If he can devour a mighty haunch of boar,' said an old song, 'and in two gulps drain a barrel of wine, pity the man on whom he wages war!'

invaders depended so much on horses that they seemed like 'shaggy centaurs' to their enemies. (Centaurs were creatures of myth: half-man, half-horse.) But it was one thing to ride on horseback to a battle; it was quite another to *fight* from the back of a galloping horse. In fact, before about 800, it was almost impossible to stay in the saddle *and* use a weapon at the same time. So why *did* it become possible, around the time that Charlemagne ruled?

The pictures on the right give you some answers. They show a stirrup, a high-backed saddle, and an ash-wood lance; three 'inventions' which changed the face of mounted warfare. It is often hard to say exactly when an invention is made. It is easier to say when that invention comes into general use. These three were taken up in western Europe between the late 700s and about 1000. The captions explain how they made it possible for men to fight so well on their horses. 'A Frank on horseback,' said one astounded medieval writer, 'could smash a hole in the walls of Babylon!'

## Keeping an army on the land

The first men to fight on horseback were the first real knights. Squadrons of European knights could make mincemeat of most old-fashioned armies of footsoldiers. They made western Europe safe from invaders; and some of them, like the Normans, then went on conquering sprees themselves, sometimes beyond Europe (see page 10). Obviously, Europe's rulers wanted to have as many of these knights serving them as possible. But there were problems: knights had to be recruited, they had to be fitted out with armour and weapons, and, most important of all, they had to be paid in peacetime. For these knights weren't like the old able-bodied freemen, who fought in emergencies but did other jobs the rest of the time. Off-duty knights had to train for battle. They were professional warriors, specialists in the art of war. And they needed a back-up team. One modern historian compares a knight's team with the crew of a tank today (see page 4). So how was all this going to be paid for?

In the Middle Ages, wealth meant land. The more land you owned, the more wealthy and powerful you were, and the more people respected you too. The peasant families who lived on your land worked for you and provided for

*Above:* This section of the Bayeux Tapestry, from about 1070, shows mounted Norman knights in a famous battle. They are killing English footsoldiers at Hastings in 1066. Three inventions helped the Norman knight to be so successful. The stirrup (A) and the high-backed saddle (B) fixed a knight firmly to his horse. When he lunged with his long ash lance (C), he was not thrown off at the moment of impact. The knight could charge at his enemy at great speed and hit with the full weight of both himself and his horse. Notice the Normans' chainmail coats or hauberks, and also their long pointed shields (D). These helped to cover the knight's side as he charged. *Below:* This is a 12th century picture of a top-speed charge with the 'couched' lance. (Couched meant tucked firmly under the right armpit, and aimed at the enemy. The knight could still hold his shield and the horse's reins in his left hand.) After about 1100 this tactic became very common in battle. Knights also began to use heavier lances. These would not break apart when they made contact with the enemy. Can you see now why it was said that 'a Frank on horseback could smash a hole in the Walls of Babylon'?

8

sometimes the specialist warriors began life as labourers. Then, through their skill in battle, they became high-ranking knights. Thus, in the early days, knighthood was a career open to those with talent. In time, however, the knights became a fixed group of warrior-governors, or 'aristocrats'. It became harder and harder for humble men to break into this group. You were an aristocrat only if your father had been an aristocrat before you, and possibly if *his* father had been an aristocrat before him. Thus a 'closed' ruling class came into being, a small class of warrior-governors of high birth. Soon it became an *international* class. Knights all over Europe felt that they had a great deal in common. So, during the twelfth century, they started to work out an international code of conduct – the code of chivalry. The clergy decided to take a hand ...□

all your needs. Therefore it made sense for rulers to pay many of their knights with gifts of land. In return for their land, the knights had to be at the beck and call of the rulers. Let's see how this worked in England after 1066, when this system came into operation.

In 1066, Duke William I of Normandy conquered England. He took all the country's land from its old owners, then shared it out among his most important Norman followers. These leading knights – the earls and barons – did far more than just fight for their king. They also kept control of their own parts of the country in peacetime; they held their own law-courts; they served as the king's much-needed deputies. And they in turn shared out their land among some of *their* own followers. In this way, high and low knights alike were rewarded with land, and were expected to serve the king whenever he needed them in future. The whole arrangement was based on land in return for services. The bits of land granted out by the king were called fiefs or fees. The Latin word for a fief was 'feudum'. So the land-for-services arrangement became known as feudalism, or the feudal system.

## Feudal aristocrats

Everyone, from king to peasant, was supposed to have a part to play in the feudal system. People were expected to pull together – peasants labouring, clergymen praying, warriors fighting – in the face of the common enemy. This might remind you of the three groupings of medieval people described on page 5. But

Dover castle. This was one of the many strongholds which the Normans built in England after the Battle of Hastings. From his castle, a feudal warrior lord ruled in the king's name over the surrounding area.

1 Write a paragraph explaining why the title of this chapter is 'The specialists take over'. Say who the specialists were, and how they were different from the warriors who went before them.

2 What advantages did cavalrymen have over footsoldiers? Can you think of any advantages that footsoldiers might have had over cavalrymen?

3 Compare the map on page 6 with a modern atlas map of Europe. List all the modern countries, and parts of modern countries, that were Christian at the time of the invasions.

4 Imagine that you are a medieval warrior lord on the eve of a battle. Your king is worried. He asks what you will do when the enemy charges with couched lanches. What do you suggest to him?

# 3 Killing for Christ

The words in the heading above might sound odd to you. So might the phrase 'Holy War'. After all, aren't Christians supposed to be peace-lovers? If someone does them wrong, aren't they supposed to turn the other cheek? In the Middle Ages, there were no simple answers to such questions. 'A man who can think of war without great sorrow,' wrote Augustine of Hippo (354–430), 'is indeed a man dead to human feelings.' But he also wrote. 'Some crimes must be punished, and that is the reason why, according to God's commands and by lawful authority, good people must fight certain wars.' Medieval people took Augustine's writings very seriously. And they took his idea of 'righteous warfare' very seriously indeed. But what *was* a righteous war?

*Above:* A picture from the 13th century, showing Jesus Christ leading holy warriors, or crusaders.

*Left:* In this 14th-century picture, Charlemagne leads his Christian knights in a 'just' war. The town ahead of them was Agen, in France, and it was held by the Saracens. Christian writers believed that Charlemagne was 'justified' in laying siege to this town, because the Saracens were Muslims.

## The Just War

The picture above shows a scene from a righteous or 'just' war. ('Just' means a war which Christians were 'justified' in fighting.) The Emperor Charlemagne (see page 6) is leading his Christian knights against the Saracen invaders of Europe. Saracens were not Christian. They were Muslim. This, according to writers who came after Augustine, made them the natural enemies of all true Christian knights. In the same way, Magyars and Vikings, who were also pagans, were natural enemies. Thus it was not wrong to fight wars against these peoples – especially when they were trying to invade Christian lands.

Medieval clergymen encouraged the knights to defend Christendom against the pagans. This was partly for selfish reasons: the churches and monasteries of western Europe were full of treasures – and this made them obvious targets for pagans in search of plunder. At first, clergymen tried to make knights do penance if they killed a pagan during a just war. But they also told knights that God was happy for them to fight. In fact, just by fighting pagans, a knight could expect rewards in the afterlife. Later in this book, you will see how that sort of thinking helped to launch the great crusades.

Some clergymen actually went as far as fighting in battles themselves. Abbots and bishops held fiefs from their rulers, and so they were expected to do military service in return. Bishop Odo of Bayeux, for example, fought in William the Conqueror's Norman army at the Battle of Hastings. Such clergymen were not, however, supposed to shed blood. They got around this by using a weapon called the mace, with which they clubbed their enemies to death rather than cut them!

## Taming the beasts

Medieval knights were therefore free to fight pagans. But what if there were no pagans to fight? What did the knights do then? One answer, unfortunately, was that they fought among themselves. This was hardly surprising. They were professional warriors, highly trained to do battle; often they chose to settle their own quarrels by taking up arms. 'Private warfare' of this kind was a way of asking God to decide who was in the right; God, it was believed, would not let the wrong man win. But private warfare could cause chaos inside a ruler's realm. And rulers had little chance of keeping their knights in check. After all, the knights themselves were the main law-enforcement officers! So, once again, the clergy tried to lay down some rules and regulations.

From the late 900s onwards, the Church tried to enforce the 'Peace of God'. This meant asking local knights to promise never to harm clergymen, or church property, or unarmed people. Then, after about 1040, bishops came up with an even better idea. It was called the 'Truce of God'. In 1095, Pope Urban II declared a Truce of God for the whole of Christendom. These were its terms:

66 Monks, clergymen, women, and those who may be with them, shall remain in peace every day; on three days of the week, that is the second, third and fourth days, an injury done to anyone shall not be considered to be breaking the peace; but on the remaining four days, if any one injures another, he shall be considered a violator of the Sacred Peace, and shall be punished in the manner decreed. 99

Sunday was the first day of the week. So that left just sunup Monday to Wednesday sundown for fighting. Needless to say, this did not seem long enough to some knights – so they ignored the Truce terms completely. But at least the Church was making an effort to tame the warlike knights (and, as the extract shows, warlike monks and women too!).

*Above:* This Flemish picture shows a knight in disgrace. He has failed to behave in a chivalrous way, and is being paraded in public for his sins.

## Preparing to serve God

The Church also became very important in the ceremony of making young men into knights. Back in the Dark Ages, an older knight would simply present the young man with a sword, then both sword and sheath would be 'girded' around his waist. Finally, the older knight would 'dub' the young man. This was a blow to the face of cheek, to remind the young man of his oaths to be a good knight. No clergyman needed to be present at all.

But by about 950, this prayer was sometimes said over the new knight's sword:

The 'Grace of God', in the form of a woman, arms a knight.

11

66Hearken, we beseech Thee, O Lord, to our prayers, and bless with the right hand of Thy majesty this sword with which this Thy servant desires to be girded. Let this sword be a defence to churches, widows, orphans and all Thy servants against the scourge of the pagans, let it be the terror and dread of other evildoers, and let it be just both in attack and defence.99

It was quite usual for clergymen to bless the tools of tradesmen. Now they were blessing the swords of the knights. And, as you can see, those swords were only to be used for 'chivalrous' purposes. (Compare these purposes with those mentioned on page 4.)

In time, a whole service grew out of this blessing. It is described in detail below by Geoffrey Charny. Not *all* new knights were made in this way. Charny wrote in the fourteenth century, quite late in the Age of Chivalry. And he is describing the knighting of a great feudal lord's son, in time of peace. As the bottom picture on page 13 shows, courageous young men were sometimes knighted on the field of battle, with no clergymen present at all. But this extract is full of information on the *Christian* code of chivalry:

66When someone is to be knighted, he should first of all confess his sins and put himself into a fit state to receive communion. And on the eve of the day when he is to be knighted, he should wash and cleanse his body of all the filth and sin of evil living, and leave his filth behind in the water. Then he should go and lie in a brand-new bed with clean white sheets and should rest and sleep there like one who has come through many torments by devils ...

Then the knights should come to the bed to dress him; and he should be dressed in new linen clothing and everything else should be new; just as his body has been washed of filth and sin, so the new clothes signify that he should keep himself clean and spotless of sin in future. Then he should be dressed by the knights in scarlet robes, to show that he is sworn to shed his blood for the faith of Our Lord and to defend and keep the laws of Holy Church. And then the knights should bring black hose, to show that he came from earth, and to earth he must return, and that he must expect to die,

*Above:* Taking the bath of knighthood.

*Below:* These knights are eating the bread of Holy Communion, before going into battle. Holy Communion is a Christian way of remembering Jesus's Last Supper with his disciples, before he was crucified.

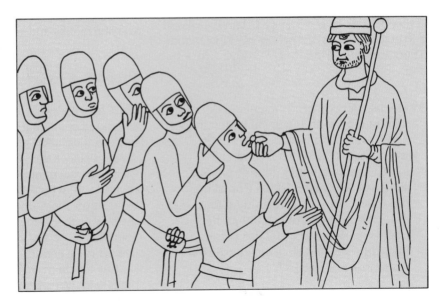

nor can he know the hour of his death, and so he must trample on all pride. Then the knights should bring a white girdle and gird it on him, as a sign that he should always be surrounded by chastity and cleanliness. Then the knights bring a scarlet cloak and put it on his shoulders as a sign of humility.

Then the knights lead him joyfully to the church, where he must remain all night until dawn in deep devotion and praying to our Lord to forgive his evil sleeping and waking the past, and to make him always watchful in his service thereafter.🙶

Quite a complicated business, then. And all that was just the preparation! On the following day, the real ceremony of knighthood would begin ...

## God's warrior

🙶The next day the knights take him to hear Mass, praying to our Lord for grace to enter the order of knighthood. And when Mass has been sung and said, the knights shall bring him to the knight who is to do the knighting. This knight shall put a gilded spur on his foot, showing that just as gold is the most desired metal, so it is put on his foot to take away all greed and desire from his heart. Then the knight who is to give him the order of knighthood girds him with a sword; just as the sword has two cutting edges, so he must keep right, reason and justice on all sides and never betray the Christian faith or the rights of Holy Church. Then the other knight kisses him, as a sign of peace and love and loyalty, which he should always seek out wherever he may rightly do so. And then that knight gives him the accolade, a blow which signifies that he must always remember the order of knighthood which he has received, and must perform the deeds which belong to the order of knighthood. And in this manner these things are and should be done.🙶

Thus did a keen young warrior enter the order of knights. But before he was ready to go through a ceremony like this, he had to serve a long apprenticeship. You can read all about it in the next section. ☐

Here the make-believe knight Galahad is being 'girded' with his sword in a church. The sword would have been brought from the altar, and blessed by the priest.

1 Explain the following terms in your own words: Holy Communion; dubbing; Just War; The Truce of God; girding.

2 Look at the top picture on page 10. Why do you think Christ has a sword between his teeth? What do you think he is holding?

3 Look closely at the picture of the knight in disgrace on page 11. Pretend you are one of the onlookers, and write a letter to a friend, describing exactly what you saw. Include some suggestions on what the knight might have *done*, to deserve his disgrace.

4 Imagine that you are a young medieval man. You have just gone through the long ceremony of knighthood described on pages 12 and 13. Describe exactly how you feel at the end of it, and say how you intend to behave from now on.

This picture is based on a 14th-century drawing. It shows a successful warrior being knighted on the battlefield itself. The standing lord touches the warrior's shoulder or neck with the flat of his sword. This was called 'dubbing'. As the Age of Chivalry went on, it became common to knight warriors on the eve of battles.

# 4 The apprentice knight

*Above:* A young squire, still learning the ins and outs of knighthood.

*Right:* A squire would first learn to use a lance on foot. Then he might learn to 'tilt at the quintain'. To tilt meant to ride and thrust with a lance. The quintain was a target which went round and round on a wooden arm.

*Right:* A squire serving at table in his lord's household. Humble tasks like this were an important part of his training. In 1275–6, the Spaniard Ramon Llull wrote this advice to a young squire: 'Seek not noble courage in speech, for speech is not always truth; see it not in rich clothes, for many fine clothes hide cowardice, treachery and evil … seek it not in fine harness and equipment for they too often hide an evil and cowardly heart. Seek noble courage in faith, hope, charity, justice, strength, moderation and loyalty'.

The dashing young man on the left is a squire or esquire. You may have heard that second word before. Today people writing letters sometimes put 'esquire' after a man's name when they address the envelope. The word actually comes from 'escuyer', the French word for shield-carrier. In the Middle Ages, a squire was a young man who carried a knight's shield for him, and also served him in other ways. This service became a kind of apprenticeship for knighthood. At the end of it, the squire himself was made a knight. But the apprenticeship was a long one, and it was much more than a simple military training. It was, in fact, a full preparation for the world of chivalry.

## A strange education

In the Middle Ages there were no schools like the ones we know today. Very few boys and girls had any schooling at all. The son of a knight was possibly given some lessons by the women in his home until he was about seven. Then he would probably be sent to another knightly castle. There he would live and work as a page, helping to run his new lord's household. At the same time he would learn the first lessons of knighthood – how to handle horses and weapons, and how to behave in a chivalrous way. By the age of 14, provided that he was shaping up well, he might at last become a squire …

Now to find out the duties of a squire, we can go back to the *Canterbury Tales* of Geoffrey Chaucer. Do you remember his 'perfect gentle knight' on page 5? Well, not surprisingly, that knight had a young squire attending on him:

> He had his son with him, a fine young
> Squire,
> A lover and cadet, a lad of fire
> With locks as curly as if they had been
> pressed
> He was some twenty years of age, I
> guessed.

Chaucer then went on to describe the young man. First he mentioned how well-qualified he was as a warrior:

> In stature he was of a moderate length,
> With wonderful agility and strength.
> He'd seen some service with the cavalry
> In Flanders and Artois and Picardy
> And had done valiantly in little space
> Of time, in hope to win his lady's
> grace.

Clearly this squire was making a good name for himself. Already he had been involved in warfare. He would have taken part in some of the fighting, but he would also have looked after his lord's horses and equipment during the heat of battle. (Remember that escuyer meant 'shield-carrier'.) He *had* to be agile and strong, in order to move around while wearing his heavy armour. He also had to be able to charge with his lance straight at an enemy, yet stay in his saddle at the moment of impact. These skills could only be perfected by practice (see picture). As for the squire being a 'lover' hoping to 'win his lady's grace', you can learn more about *that* side of things on page 23! Chaucer then went on to list the squire's more peaceable features:

> ❝He was embroidered like a meadow bright
> And full of freshest flowers, red and white
> Singing he was, or fluting all the day;
> He was as fresh as is the month of May.
> Short was his gown, the sleeves were long and wide;
> He knew the way to sit a horse and ride.
> He could make songs and poems and recite,
> Knew how to joust and dance, to draw and write.
> He loved so hotly that till dawn grew pale
> He slept as little as a nightingale.❞

So this young squire was like a chivalrous knight in miniature. He was fashionably dressed, and skilled in several arts, as well as being a highly-trained killer. He was even able to tell a long tale to the rest of Chaucer's pilgrims on the road to Canterbury. But, until he was actually knighted, he was still mainly a servant:

> ❝Courteous he was, lowly and serviceable,
> And carved to serve his father at the table.❞

He might expect to be made a knight around the age of 21. If he was lucky, he would receive a grant of land at the same time. The income from this land would cover the expenses of knighthood (see page 16). But not all young knights *did* receive grants immediately, so they had to finance themselves in other ways. These 'knights bachelor' could look for wealthy heiresses to marry. Or they could become

'mercenaries', warriors who fought for whoever would pay them. Such knights lived only for warfare. And when there were no wars to fight in, they sharpened their skills with 'mimic warfare', at the tournaments . . . ☐

Here a squire is helping to arm his lord before battle. This could be a lengthy job, and the armour could weigh as much as 55 lbs. It is no wonder that one poet called the medieval knight: 'a terrible worm in an iron cocoon'!

1  Read again Chaucer's description of the young squire on pages 14 and 15. Then draw and colour your own strip cartoon of him, showing him doing four of the things mentioned in the poem.

2  What was a quintain? How do you think the quintain in the picture on page 14 worked?

3  In what ways would you have a) liked, b) not liked being a medieval squire?

# 5 The tale of the tourney

A mêlée at a 15th century tournament. You had to be rich to take part. Horses and armour were very expensive; knights were expected to show *largesse* to heralds, minstrels, grooms, squires and armourers; and if a knight was captured, he had to pay his own ransom.

" A knight cannot shine in war if he has not prepared for it in tournaments. He must have seen his own blood flow, have had his teeth crunched under the blow of his opponent, have been dashed to the earth with such force as to feel the weight of his foe, and been disarmed twenty times; he must twenty times have made good his failures, more keen than ever upon the combat. Then will he be able to confront actual war with the hope of being victorious. " *(Roger de Hoveden)*

These are the words of a twelfth century-chronicler. That was the time when tournaments became popular all over Europe. As you can see from the picture, they were practice battles, and sometimes it was hard to tell them apart from real warfare. An eleventh-century French knight called Godfrey de Preuilly is said to have invented the tournament; English chroniclers referred to it as 'French conflict'. But in fact similar warlike games were played by Frankish warriors as long ago as the ninth century. Soldiers of all centuries need to keep themselves ready for war with battle-practice. But tournaments, or tourneys, became much more than simple training-sessions for young knights and mercenaries. They offered the chance to win great fame and great riches, and they turned into the most dazzling spectator sport of the Middle Ages.

## 'Mimic warfare'

William Marshal was a poor young knight who made a name for himself at the tourneys. In the 1170s and 1180s, he travelled far and wide to take part in them, fighting in the company of his feudal lord, Prince Henry of England. These tourneys were organized by wealthy European rulers and nobles – they had to be wealthy, to entertain the contestants and to provide prizes for those knights who were judged to be the most skilful fighters. The tourneys were usually held in a large open space, with the contestants forming two opposing teams. Once the fight or 'mêlée' began, it was every man for himself. Often men were killed or badly wounded. Sometimes the mêlée raged way beyond the chosen site, causing havoc in the surrounding countryside. Tourney officials tried to keep some sort of order but their task was a difficult one. When the fighting was over, those who had been captured had to ransom themselves – sometimes they had to hand over their horses and armour to their captors.

You can imagine how fierce and furious the whole thing could become. And spectators turned up in droves to watch the fun.

> **❝**On either side the ranks tremble and a roar rises from the fight. The shock of lances is very great. Lances break and shields are riddled, the hauberks receive bumps and are torn asunder, saddles go empty and horsemen tumble, while the horses sweat and foam. Swords are quickly drawn on those who fall noisily, and some run to receive the promise of a ransom, others to stave off this disgrace.**❞**      *(Chrétien de Troyes, c1165)*

## Seven deadly sins

On page 11, you saw how the clergy tried to keep the knights under control. Now to their way of thinking, the tourney was little more than a 'pagan circus'. In 1130, at the Council of Clermont, Pope Innocent II condemned 'those detestable markets and fairs, vulgarly called tournaments, at which knights are wont to assemble, in order to display their strength and their rash boldness'. He also ordered that those who were killed at tourneys should not be given a Christian burial. This order didn't have much effect. In fact the ban was eventu-

ally lifted in 1316. The tourneys were just too popular for the Church to interfere with them.

But clergymen continued to complain. Jacques de Vitry tried to explain that tourneys led knights to commit all seven deadly sins, in this way:

1   Pride – because the contestants compete for the praise of men;
2   Hate and Anger – because they often seek revenge and commit murder;
3   Depression – because some contestants fare badly or are injured;
4   Greed – because they aim to take one another's horses and armour;
5   Gluttony – because they eat and drink too much at the final feasts;
6   Vanity – because they put earthly matters before religious ones;
7   Lechery – because they fight to catch the eye of 'wanton' women. (Do you remember Chaucer's squire on page 15, 'hoping to win his lady's grace'?)

Some knights must have paid heed to this kind of warning. But they took a little more notice when their own kings and princes started to lay down the law . . .

This 15th-century picture shows a tourney in the presence of King Arthur. You can find out more about the legendary Arthur on pages 23 to 25. Real-life kings like Edward I of England held 'Round Tables', like the one at Nefyn in Wales in 1284. At these events there was jousting, and festivities like those at the court of King Arthur.

## Taking the sting out of tourneys

Europe's rulers weren't worried about the knights' souls. They were much more concerned with the practical problems caused by tourneys. For one thing, they didn't like the great lords gathering together, with all their own supporters: tourneys are ideal places to hatch plots and rebellions against rulers. But those rulers were also worried about the sheer loss of life. It seemed so wasteful to lose their most valuable warriors in *mock* battles ...

At Cologne in 1240, for example, 60 knights were killed. At Neuss in 1241 80 were said to have died. And a French tourney in 1273 became so chaotic that it was remembered as 'the little battle of Châlons'. Obviously, tourneys could pose a threat to law and order. They were also suitable places to carry on private feuds. One ruler after another tried to ban them. But, just as the knights ignored the Church's warnings, so they ignored the rulers' threats. Nevertheless, the rulers were more successful in making the tourneys better-organized – and safer.

In England, King Richard I (1189–99), tried to limit tourneys rather than ban them altogether. According to William of Newburgh, he did this because he saw that the French 'were fiercer and better trained for war ... and he did not wish to see the French mock the knights of his own kingdom for rudeness and lack of skill.' But it was King Edward I (1272–1307) who laid down the strictest rules and regulations for tourneys.

---

**Edward's Law of 1294**

1 No sharp weapons were to be carried, by contestants or spectators.
2 No earl, baron or knight was to bring more than three squires.
3 If a contestant was knocked off his horse, only his squire was allowed to raise him up.
4 A committee of stewards would make sure that the rules were kept.
5 If anyone broke the rules, he would be sent to jail.
6 At any tourney feasts, numbers of guests would be strictly controlled.

---

Gradually, similar rules were coming into force throughout Europe. The timetable above right shows exactly what went on at a tourney at Chauvency in France in 1285. As you can see, it was highly-organized; more like a theatrical event than a free-for-all fight. It was still dangerous enough to delight the spectators, but much safer than in the past. And this was partly because 'jousting' was becoming more important than the general mêlée ...

## The civilized joust

The old mêlée had been like a miniature war between two sides. The joust was a single combat between champions. In some ways it was like a mock duel. There were a number of 'courses' to be fought with different weapons. To begin with, the contestants charged at each other several times with lances. Points were scored for knocking an opponent off his horse,

*Below:* In October 1285, the Count of Chimy put on a tournament at Chauvency in north-eastern France. A minstrel called Jacques Bretel was there. He wrote a full account of what happened, and this timetable has been taken from it.

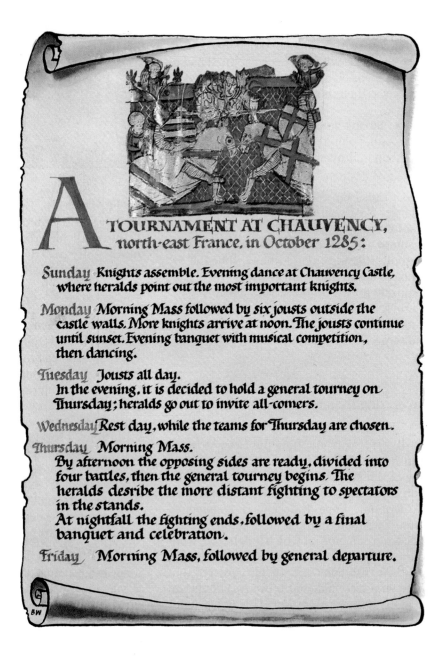

A TOURNAMENT AT CHAUVENCY, north-east France, in October 1285:

**Sunday** Knights assemble. Evening dance at Chauvency Castle, where heralds point out the most important knights.

**Monday** Morning Mass followed by six jousts outside the castle walls. More knights arrive at noon. The jousts continue until sunset. Evening banquet with musical competition, then dancing.

**Tuesday** Jousts all day.
In the evening, it is decided to hold a general tourney on Thursday; heralds go out to invite all-comers.

**Wednesday** Rest day, while the teams for Thursday are chosen.

**Thursday** Morning Mass.
By afternoon the opposing sides are ready, divided into four battles, then the general tourney begins. The heralds describe the more distant fighting to spectators in the stands.
At nightfall the fighting ends, followed by a final banquet and celebration.

**Friday** Morning Mass, followed by general departure.

or, more usually, for splintering his lance. (In one kind of German jousting, if a shield was hit in the middle, a spring inside it was released, and the shield flew apart over the jouster's head!) Then the contestants would dismount to exchange blows with swords, and an axe-fight might follow. The contest could end when one man fell exhausted, or when one had scored a certain number of points. Often the weapons themselves were tipped or blunted. But even if they were not, the contestants were better protected by new plate armour, instead of the chainmail hauberks of old. All in all, these contests were a lot more civilized than the brutal mêlées.

## 'Soft tournies'

The question was: were these jousts a good way to prepare for real warfare? Some critics thought that they weren't. Henri de Laon wrote that tourneys were becoming too soft, too much like pure entertainment. Indeed, the new tourneys were really tests of individual skill, not practice for teamwork on the battle-field. As you will see on page 30, warfare changed a lot between 1100 and 1400. This left the mounted knights looking somewhat out of date. But at the tourneys, they carried on acting out their fantasies of chivalry. And sometimes those fantasies could be very colourful indeed. These kind of tournaments were still being held as late as the sixteenth century. Long before that time, however, they had become no more than lavish pageants, harmless except for the occasional accident.

But in their heyday, writes the historian Barbara Tuchman, tournaments were:

66the peak of nobility's pride and delight
in its own valour and beauty ... with
brilliantly-dressed spectators in the
stands, flags and ribbons fluttering, the
music of trumpets, the parade of
combatants making their draped horses
prance and champ on golden bridles,
the glitter of harness and shields, the
throwing of ladies' scarves and sleeves
to their favourites, the bow of the
heralds to the presiding prince who
proclaimed the rules ...99

These last-named men, the heralds, became extremely important at the tourneys. It's worth taking a look at them now. For the Age of Chivalry would have been quite different without them ...□

Ulrich von Lichtenstein, a 13th-century jouster and poet from Styria. At one time he dressed up as King Arthur and rode with six companions through Austria and Styria writing poems and jousting. He wrote of his adventures. But what he wrote owes more to imagination than fact.

*Below:* This 15th-century picture shows a display at a French tournament. The flags show the colours of those knights who were taking part. As you can see, women as well as men were interested in the display.

1  a) Write a paragraph, describing in your own words what is happening in the picture on page 16. b) Write a paragraph describing the clothing of Ulrich von Lichtenstein and his horse in the top picture on page 19.

2  Why do you think medieval tournaments were so popular with a) knights and b) spectators? Why do you think they were so unpopular with c) clergymen and d) rulers?

# 6 Heraldry: art and science

❝**D**o you see that knight yonder with a golden band across his red shield? That is Governauz of Roberdic. And do you see that other one, who has an eagle and a dragon painted side by side on his shield? That is the son of the King of Aragon, who has come to this land in search of glory and renown. And do you see that other one beside him, who thrusts and jousts so well, bearing a shield with a leopard painted on a green ground on one part, on the other azure blue? That is Ignaures the well-beloved . . .❞ *(Chrétien de Troyes)*

Nowadays, every player in a professional football team wears the same colours. This serves two purposes. It helps the crowd to tell from a distance which team is which. It also helps the players themselves to tell in the heat of the moment who is on their side and who isn't. Tourneys, not football matches, were the big spectator sports of the Middle Ages. And, as the paragraph above shows, tourney crowds picked out their heroes by their colours too. Instead of 'kit', the knights had personal patterns or 'devices' on their shields. Sometimes they also wore the same devices on the crests of their helmets, their surcoats, and on the drapery of their horses (see picture). These devices could be very artistic, but they were more than mere decorations. In those days, there were no military uniforms. So, in the heat of battle, the devices helped the knights to tell their friends from their foes.

## The business of blazon

The knights in the picture are displaying their coat of arms or 'heraldic' devices. It seems that knights began to wear such devices around the year 1140. Warriors had been using banners and emblems for a long time before then – but only for themselves. True heraldic devices, however, were passed on from one generation to the next. In this way, coats of arms belonged to whole families, not just to individuals. And they were used on glass, on building-stones and on tombs, as well as on shields. They were also used to seal important letters. This was particularly useful, since many members of the knightly order were quite unable to read!

*Left:* Knights jousting in their own colours, hoping to win their ladies' favours. 'If at arms you excel (do well), you will be ten times loved' said a medieval poem, the *Romance of the Rose.*

*Below:* These were the Nine Worthies – the greatest heroes of medieval times. They were: Joshua, David and Judas Maccabeus from the Bible; Hector, Alexander the Great and Julius Caesar from pagan times; Arthur, Charlemagne and Godfrey of Bouillon from Christian times. Medieval heralds made up special coats of arms for them all.

Arms came to play a vital part in medieval life. Obviously no two families wanted to have the same arms. So it became very important to describe your arms clearly – and claim them for yourself alone. This was where the science of 'blazon' came in. The pictures on the right tell you all about it. The captions include some of the heraldic language which was used for

THE COLOURS

Gules     Vert     Azure     Sable

THE METALS

Argent     Or

THE CHARGES

Bend     Fess     Saltire     Chevron

THE DIVISIONS

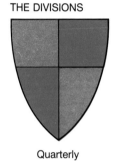 

Quarterly     Paly

describing arms. Some of the words might sound peculiar to you – 'gules' for red, 'vair' for squirrel fur, and so on. They were Norman French, not English, and they have remained in that language ever since.

From around 1250, records or 'rolls' of arms were being kept in England and France. They stuck closely to the rules of blazon. There could, however, still be bitter disputes. In 1385 Sir Richard Scrope and Sir Robert Grosvenor appeared at a tourney wearing the same arms – 'azure à bend or' (gold bend on a blue ground). After a great uproar, the Marshal and Constable decided in favour of Scrope, and told Grosvenor to find himself a new coat of arms. Today the Grosvenor arms show a golden wheatsheaf. But the old quarrel wasn't forgotten for centuries. In fact the family of the 2nd Grosvenor Duke of Westminster called their famous racehorse 'Bend Or' – and the Duke himself come to be known by that name too!

## The right to bear arms

As you can imagine, aristocratic families grew very proud of their arms. Sometimes their devices were highly complicated, and told stories of the chivalrous deeds of long-dead relatives. In 1386 Sir Robert Laton described how his father had educated him in chivalry –

partly by writing down and learning the arms of princes, barons and knights.

Men and women could also be snobbish about 'lesser' families, who didn't have the right to bear arms. Yet who exactly *was* allowed to bear arms? The answer wasn't as straightforward as you might think. The *Boke of St Albans* (1486) said that a man could claim arms on four grounds:

1 because he inherited them;
2 because they went with a particular fief or job;
3 because a lord or prince granted them to him;
4 because he captured them from an enemy in battle.

But even in the fifteenth century, 'many poor men' were taking arms simply because they wanted to do so. This annoyed the 'true' nobles enormously. They believed that arms were closely linked with the matter of honour. As the Spaniard Diego de Valera put it:

66 On the day of battle, every noble knight and esquire should wear his coat of arms ... and the purpose of this is that those who are noble should be known among the common soldiery, and that they should be reminded that it is their duty not to bring disgrace upon themselves and their ancestors ... 99

There were certain clear rules in the art of blazon. The colours and metals shown above (red, green, blue, black, silver and gold) were used for the backgrounds of shields. Then the charges (bend, fess, saltire, chevron) show some of the ways in which you could add to these backgrounds. You could not put a colour charge upon a colour background, or a metal upon a metal. It had to be a metal upon a colour or *vice versa*. Finally there were the divisions, some more complicated grounds for decorating shields. Only two, quarterly and paly, are shown here.

*Above:* Heralds in a procession to a 16th-century tournament. An apprentice herald was called a pursuivant. In time he became a herald, and then, if he was successful, A King of Arms. There is still a College of Arms in London today, for dealing with heraldic matters.

*Right:* A rubbing of a brass memorial in Blickling, Norfolk. It shows Sir Nicholas Dagworth who died in 1401, along with his personal coats of arms.

# The rise of the heralds

All branches of learning have their experts. The experts in the science of blazon, the 'officers of arms', were called heralds. Their kind of work came to be known as heraldry. In ancient times, heralds were officers who made public proclamations and arranged ceremonies. By the early Middle Ages, they were often simply messengers, serving particular lords on the battlefield. Then, around the year 1200, they seem to have become specialists at identifying knights by their coats of arms. They also learned by heart the chivalrous feats of those knights. These skills were extremely useful at tourneys. On page 18, you saw how important the heralds were at the Chauvency tourney of 1285. By that time, the job of a herald was quite a good one to have. He wore the arms of his lord, he was paid for his work, and, after serving his apprenticeship as a 'pursuivant', he could look forward to being made a 'King of Arms' one day.

Over the next two centuries, the heralds were given more and more duties. At tourneys they inspected the arms of those who wished to take part – and made sure that they were of truly noble blood. Then they kept a close count of the points scored in the jousts. They were also the men who knew exactly how to organize coronations and other great ceremonies. Meanwhile, they were needed during real warfare too. They stood on the sidelines at battles, with their safety guaranteed, and recorded knightings and feats of arms. Afterwards, medieval chroniclers used these records as sources when they wrote their historical books.

Heralds had one other interesting side to their work. They were meant to serve 'all gentlewomen'. According to the Anjou King of Arms, they had a duty to carry messages between 'honorable lovers' and also keep their secrets. Women had a very important part to play in the world of the knights. Let's take a closer look now at the more romantic side of chivalry ... □

1  Using reference books, find out about any *three* of the Nine Worthies, and write a paragraph on each. Say why you think they were once so popular.

2  Using the information in the pictures on page 21, draw and colour in shields showing i) azure à bend or; ii) a suitable background and charge for yourself, remembering to obey the rules of blazon.

# 7 Legends, ladies and lovers

History is meant to be about things that really happened. But as you might have noticed, some of the extracts in this book come from medieval *fiction*. Some of the pictures too show make-believe men and women, not real ones. There is a good reason for all this. In the Middle Ages, people didn't see things in the way that we do today. They had different ideas about what was true or not true. Medieval people weren't necessarily *more stupid* than we are. But they were more ready to believe stories about marvels and monsters and heroes. And sometimes they tried to live their own lives like the characters in the stories. In this way fiction had an effect on the way people behaved. And it affected medieval knights more than almost anyone else . . .

Roland lies dead after the Battle of Roncesvalles, but two angels take his soul to heaven. Roland's heroic deeds were famous for centuries. According to the *Song of Roland* he had a sword called Durandaal and a horse called Veillantif.

## Songs of deeds

**❝**The Prince Grandoyne was a good
  knight and gallant,
  Strong of his hands and valorous in
  battle;
  Against him now comes Roland the
  great captain . . .
  He cannot help it, a mortal fear runs
  through him;
  Fain would he fly, but what's the good?
  he cannot.
  The count assails him with such
  ferocious valour
  That to the nasal the whole helmet is
  shattered,
  Cloven to the nose and the teeth and
  the palate,
  The jaz'rain hauberk and the breast-
  bone and backbone,
  Both silver bows off the golden saddle;
  Horseman and horse clean asunder he
  slashes,
  Lifeless he leaves them and the pieces
  past patching.
  The men of Spain fall a-wailing for
  sadness:
  The French all cry: "What strokes! and
  what a champion!"**❞**

That comes from *The Song of Roland*, a French epic poem written in the eleventh century. In real life, Roland had been a knight at the court

of Charlemagne. Thanks to the poem, he became a French national hero. Frenchmen saw him as the perfect warrior – brave, loyal, sworn to fight for Christ against the infidel Saracens. Knights everywhere loved to hear tales of fearless heroes like Roland. The more bloodthirsty they were, the better! So poets made up 'chansons de geste' – songs of deeds – for them to listen to. Then the knights could dream of acting out similar deeds themselves. The chansons thus inspired the knights, and guided them along the path of true knighthood.

## Three Great Matters

Stories about Charlemagne and his Frankish court became popular in many countries. They were known as the Matter of France. Tales of ancient Romans, Trojans and Greeks became popular too – especially stories about Alexander the Great. These were known as the Matter of Rome the Great. But from about the middle of the twelfth century, there was a third Great Matter. It featured the wonderful adventures of King Arthur and his Knights of the Round Table, and it was called the Matter of Britain. Arthur may or may not have existed in real life. But people in Britain and Europe were telling stories about him long before they were first written down. Poets turned the old legends into new stories called 'romances of chivalry'.

The romances were enormously popular in the courts and castles of Europe. Men like Ulrich von Lichtenstein actually modelled themselves on Arthur's gallant knights (see page 19). In England, special tourneys called 'Round Tables' were held. It became quite hard to tell fact from fiction. But the education of both squires and heralds had to include a study of the romances. And in time, the romances helped to shape the code of chivalry.

## 'The recognition of noble women'

The chansons had been mainly about warriors and warfare. Women hardly figured in them – and neither did the more pleasant and peaceful things of life. The romances, however, dealt with passion and love and courtly matters as well as with fighting. The Matter of Britain, for example, included the tragic love story of Sir Lancelot and Queen Guinevere. This romantic trend had been started by the 'troubadours', poet-minstrels from the south of France. The trend was then continued by northern French poets called 'trouvères', and later by German knightly 'minnesingers'. Take a look at this romantic verse by Jaufré Rudel:

66 When the days grow long in May
  I love to hear the distant bird;
  When I have left off listening
  It reminds me of my distant love
  And I go dull and bent with longing
  So that song, flower and hawthorn
  Might as well be winter frosts for me. 99

Tales of Arthur and his warrior band were first told long before the Age of Chivalry. The early stories were probably pagan, not Christian, and were well known in Europe. The early 12th-century carving above comes from Modena Cathedral in Italy. On the arch Arthur, Gawain and other knights are going to the rescue of 'Winlogee' or Queen Guinevere. The French pictures below show scenes from *The Romance of Lancelot du Lac* – a heroic Arthurian poem. Arthur and his knights did not belong to Britain alone!

A Dark Age warrior would probably have called that kind of thing 'soppy'. He lived in a harsh, unsafe world – and he had little time for gentle thoughts. But by the end of the twelfth century, life was becoming more settled in Europe. The barbarian hordes were no longer a threat. And some knights began to see that there was more to life than killing, drinking, feasting and boasting! Therefore they enjoyed verses of this sort, by Bernart de Ventadorn:

> 66 Noble lady, I ask of you
> To take me as your servitor;
> I'll serve you as I would my lord,
> Whatever my reward shall be.
> Look, I am here at your command,
> You who are noble, gay and kind. 99

In the great romances, knights really *did* serve women. They went on long journeys, seeking to test themselves, to prove that they were worthy of their chosen mistresses. This was a far cry indeed from the older medieval attitude to women (see picture).

Knights now began to take love very seriously. They believed that loving a woman would inspire them to achieve great deeds. It didn't matter if the women didn't love them back. In fact the women were almost always married to other men, just as Lancelot's Guinevere was married to King Arthur! (Most feudal marriages were business arrangements, not love-matches. And, as Benjamin Franklin once pointed out, 'where there is marriage without love, there will be love without marriage.')

This 'courtly love', as it was called, was very complicated and sometimes rather silly (see caption on the right). But thanks mainly to the literature of chivalry, European men started treating their womenfolk with more respect. And this in turn made the men more civilized and courteous. Of course, some knights remained rough and raw and unfit for anything expect fighting. But others took the lessons of the romances to heart. The chronicler Froissart wrote that in 1340 there were some young English knights in Flanders. All of them wore a patch over one eye. Each one had sworn to see with just one eye, until he had performed a heroic feat of arms worthy of his lady! Another character, in a German romance, declared on the eve of a battle: 'There are two rewards that await us – heaven, and the recognition of noble women.' And now we turn to some knights who were more interested in the first reward than the second – the crusaders ... □

A man beating his wife, an illustration from the *Romance of the Rose*. Some medieval men did not think highly of women. 'Look Girbers', says a character in one book, pointing out a girl, 'look at that beauty'. 'You would do better,' replied Girbers, 'to look at the beautiful beast of a horse I have here'. Compare this with the picture and caption below.

A young woman gives her heart to the knight she has chosen. Just before 1200, in *The Art of Courtly Love* Andreas Capellanus laid down these rules: 'Marriage is no real excuse for not loving'; 'He who is not jealous cannot love'; 'When it stops being secret, love rarely lasts'; 'A man in love is always fearful'; 'Nothing forbids one woman being loved by two men or one man by two women'.

1   Explain the following terms: chansons de geste; courtly love; troubadours; the Matter of Britain.

2   Look closely at the pictures on the bottom right of page 24. Then write a short story based on what you think is happening in the pictures. Be sure to make your story as exciting as possible – and remember that the *woman* in the story must be important.

3   Do you think that any of the 'rules' of courtly love (in the caption on the right) are true today? Have a class discussion about them.

# 8 Crusaders and military monks

"We have heard that a new sort of chivalry has appeared on earth, and in that region which Christ himself once visited ... I say that this is a new sort of chivalry, unknown through the centuries, because it tirelessly wages an equal and double war, both against flesh and blood and against the spiritual forces of evil in the other world."

(*Bernard of Clairvaux, c. 1130*)

These words refer to the Knights of the Temple, or Templars. Their organization or 'order' was set up soon after 1100, in the land that is now called Israel. Bernard was quite right – there had never been anything like the Templars before. They were feudal warriors who vowed to become monks, so that they could wage a holy war on the Muslims. But what were the Templars – and other orders like them – doing in Israel, the Holy Land? To answer that, we must take a look at the great medieval crusades ...

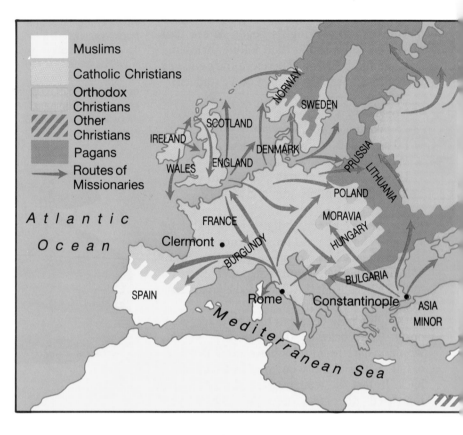

*Above:* Europe after the Dark Ages. There were Christians of several different kinds. Christian missionaries converted pagans in the east. But the Muslim faith was mighty too, especially in the Middle East – which the Christians called *their* Holy Land.

## The First Crusade and after

You already know that the Church tried to keep a check on the knights (see pages 11 and 17). During the Dark Ages, it encouraged them to fight in defence of the Christian religion. But compare the map of Europe in *c.* 800 (on page 6) with the map above showing Europe in *c.* 1100. There were still 'infidels' to fight in Spain, and pagans around the Baltic Sea. But elsewhere in Europe, there were few places where knights could fight the good fight. This meant that they tended to fight more often among themselves – and the Church strongly disapproved of this. So, in 1095, Pope Urban II made a great speech at Clermont in France. 'Let those who have been robbers now be soldiers of Christ,' he proclaimed, 'let those who have been mercenaries for a few pieces of silver now win an eternal reward.' What did he want the knights to do? He wanted them to travel out of Europe, and reclaim the Holy Land from its Muslim overlords!

And that was exactly what they did. The story of that first crusade is almost unbeliev-able. It ended with the international army of European knights capturing Jerusalem, and setting up four feudal states of their own. But it was one thing to conquer these lands – and quite another to defend them against the neighbouring Muslim states. More and more crusaders were needed from Europe. Clergy-men like Bernard of Clairvaux appealed to their sense of chivalry in this way:

"O mighty soldier, O man of war, you now have a cause for which you can fight without endangering your soul; a cause in which to win is glorious and for which to die is but gain. Or are you a shrewd businessman, a man quick to see the profits of this world? If you are, I can offer you a splendid bargain. Do not miss this opportunity. Take the sign of the cross. At once you will have indulgence [*forgiveness*] for all the sins which you confess with a contrite [*sorry*] heart. It does not cost you much to buy, and if you wear it with humility you will find that it is worth the kingdom of heaven."

*Above:* The seal of the Templars.

Plenty of European men snapped up Bernard's 'splendid bargain'. A great number of them were French, but there were English crusaders too, like King Richard the Lionheart (1189–99). These warriors went on expeditions to help out the crusader states, then returned to Europe. They believed that they belonged to a truly international brotherhood of chivalry – despite the frequent quarrels between them! But the states needed more permanent defenders too –soldiers who would always be ready to fight in any emergency. This was where the religious orders of knighthood came in . . .

## Monks of war

The pictures show three of the most important orders: the Templars, the Knights of St John (or Knights Hospitallers), and the Teutonic Knights. As you can see from the captions, they were all formed for different reasons. But members of all three orders were supposed to live and worship God just like monks, remain unmarried, and obey their Grand Masters in all matters. They were meant to dedicate their whole lives to serving God – and that meant fighting non-Christians for the most part. Thus the orders became highly-organized, highly-efficient military machines.

**A Knight of St John, or Knight Hospitaller.** This Order was founded at the time of the First Crusade. Its job was to protect and entertain Christian pilgrims to the Holy Sepulchre in Jerusalem. Gradually the Order became more military, and set up centres in many European countries.

**A Knight of the Temple or Templar.** This Order, based in the Temple of Solomon in Jerusalem, was officially set up in 1128. It defended and protected the holy places and the Christian pilgrims. It became enormously wealthy, owning land all over Europe, and acting as a banker.

**A Teutonic Knight.** This Order was set up in 1190, and was German in origin. Its first task was to protect and care for German pilgrims to the Holy Land. In 1198 it became a military Order. In the 13th century it turned to conquering pagan parts of eastern Europe, making them Christian.

*Left:* Templar leaders being burned in Paris in 1313. The Order had grown very rich. The Pope and other European rulers feared the Templars' power. So, for good reasons or bad, the Order was forbidden to exist any longer.

*Far left:* In this 15th-century picture, Christian crusaders marked by the red cross are doing battle with Muslim Moors in Spain. The Christians did not 'reconquer' all of Spain from the Muslims until 1492.

Obviously they fought in pitched battles. But they also garrisoned castles throughout the crusader states. And they were vitally important at sieges, in negotiating with the enemy, and in dealing with raids. In time, they came to have a large say in the governing of the states as well. Without the military orders, the Christians could not have clung on in the Holy Land for as long as they did – until 1291.

In this 14th-century French picture, crusader knights are coming face to face with Muslims in the Holy Land. The crusaders learned a great deal about warfare from the Muslims. 'Whoever has seen the Franks,' wrote Usamah, 'has found them to be creatures superior in courage and ferocity, but in nothing else, just as animals are superior in strength and aggression.'

But there was another side to the orders too. They were supposed not to care for the pleasures and luxuries of life. Bernard described the early Templars as men who 'never dress gaily, wash themselves seldom, with shaggy, tangled hair, begrimed with dust, wearing dull armour burnt up by the sun ... Their horses are not garnished with ornaments or decked with trappings, for they think of battle and victory, not pomp and show.' This was a different world from that of the courtly lovers and colourful jousters back in Europe. Yet the Templars, Hospitallers and Teutonic Knights all grew very wealthy as they grew in power. They became great landowners, in Europe as well as the Middle East. Sometimes the orders competed against each other for influence. They acted as bankers and money-lenders. The more important members were seen to live in magnificent style. For these reasons, the orders became hated and envied by many. The Templars in particular suffered a horrible fate in the end (see page 27). Nevertheless, military orders continued to do vital Chistian work, especially in Spain and the Baltic region, long after the crusader states had been wiped out.

## Chivalry in the Holy Land

The Muslims of the Middle East were puzzled by the ideas of a 'monk at war' and an 'armed pilgrim'. One twelfth-century Muslim writer, Usamah, recalled with amazement:

> 66 A Frankish knight who had just arrived from his land in order to make the holy pilgrimage ... kept constant company with me. When he decided to return to his homeland, he said: 'My brother, I am leaving for my country and I want you to send with me your son. In my country he can see the knights and learn wisdom and chivalry. When he returns, he will be like a wise man.'
>
> ... even if my son were to be taken captive, that would bring him no worse misfortune than carrying him into the lands of the Franks. However, I said to the man:
>
> 'This has exactly been my idea. Yet his grandmother ... only let him come out with me after making me swear an oath that I would return him to her.'
>
> he asked, 'Is your mother still alive?'
>
> 'Yes,' I replied.
>
> 'Well,' he said, 'do not disobey her.' 99

This says a lot about knightly ways during the Age of Chivalry. But no Age lasts forever. How did the Age of Chivalry die out? ... □

*Right:* St John's Ambulancemen attending to a runner at a sporting event. These are members of the modern-day Order of the Hospital of St John. The old Order had been stamped out in England in the 16th century, it was set up again in 1888.

1   What was Bernard of Clairvaux's 'splendid bargain'? If you had been a knight in the 12th century, would you have 'missed the opportunity' to take it? Say why, or why not, remembering to mention what (and who) you would be leaving behind.

2   Why was Usamah so amazed by the story he told on this page? What does the story tell you about the Frankish knight? What do you think Usamah thought of him?

# 9 The death of chivalry

Nowadays you might hear people saying: 'The Age of Chivalry is not dead.' They mean that some men still behave in a courteous way – usually towards women. But the real medieval code of chivalry has no place in our modern world. The idea of an international brotherhood of Christian warriors is long gone. In fact, the idea was going out of date as long ago as 1400. So the true Age of Chivalry, which began around the year 1100, didn't last very long at all. This was mainly because ways of fighting changed, and the feudal mounted knights gradually went out of fashion ...

As the Middle Ages drew on, fortifications became stronger, and long sieges became more common. Gunners were needed to blast down the walls. Knights on horseback weren't really much use. The knights in the picture have agreed to 'fight at the barriers', to help while away the time during a siege.

## Chivalry and real war

In their heyday, the chivalrous knights lived for war.

66 When you see that your quarrel is just and your blood is fighting well, tears rise to your eyes. Sweet feelings of loyalty and pity fill your heart when you see your friend so valiantly expose his body. Then you strive to live or die with him, and for love never to desert him. And from this there arises such a joy that he who has tasted it cannot even express his delight. Does such a man fear death? Not at all, for he is so strengthened, so elated, he forgets himself entirely. 99

(*Jouvencal* – the tale of Jean de Bueil's heroic deeds)

Blind King John of Bohemia sought out battles and tournaments all over Europe even *after* he had lost his eyesight! Yet warfare was not always so glamorous. Jean de Beaumont wrote this in his *Vows of the Heron*:

66 When we are in the tavern drinking strong wine, and the ladies pass and look at us, then nature urges us to have a desiring heart (for battle). But when we are on campaign on our trotting chargers, our bucklers around our necks and our lances lowered, and the great cold is congealing us together, and our limbs are crushed before and behind and our enemies are approaching us, then we would wish to be in a cellar so large that we might never be seen by any means. 99

Richard of Warwick receives the Order of the Garter (*right*) from King Henry IV in 1403. This Order was founded towards the end of the Age of Chivalry. It still exists today. The picture on the far right shows a modern ceremony of Garter knights.

# Footsoldiers make a comeback

This book began with Geoffrey Chaucer's description of the 'perfect gentle knight'. Later you read about the squire who accompanied him. Now, by the time that Chaucer was writing his *Canterbury Tales* (*c.* 1380), ways of fighting wars had changed a great deal since 1100. At the squire's side was a yeoman – and he carried a weapon which spelled disaster to the knights:

66 This Yeoman wore a coat and hood of
green,
And peacock-feathered arrows, bright
and keen
And neatly sheathed, hung at his belt
the while
– For he could dress his gear in yeoman
style.
His arrows never drooped their feathers
low –
And in his hand he bore a mighty
bow. 99

This yeoman archer also carried a shield, a sword and a short stabbing-knife. Such men were not of noble birth but humble. They fought on foot, not on horseback. But at battles such as Agincourt (1415), the mounted knights had no answer to them. The picture on this page shows you *why* the archer was so deadly. Alongside him stand a gunner, a pikeman, and a mercenary soldier – three more types of warrior who spelled disaster for the chivalrous knight. With men like these around, the mounted knights would no longer think of the battlefield as their own private playground. By the early fifteenth century the knights were still far from useless: as cavalrymen, they could still play a vital part in battles. But by then, the men-at-arms made up just one unit of an army. Fighting battles had to be a team effort, not a way of winning fame for individual deeds of prowess. The knights simply had to fit in with their fellow-soldiers, noble and humble alike.

In some ways, France had always been the true home of chivalry. French knights, French crusaders, French writers and French courtiers had set standards for other Europeans to follow. But the French were also the first to master the new, non-chivalrous warfare. French kings were quick to build up a 'national' army, completely under their own control. Gone were the days of the *international* brotherhood of Christian knights. The modern historian Michael Howard writes:

66 When Charles VIII set out for Italy in 1494, he did so with the finest army Europe had yet see: Swiss pikemen making up the core of the infantry, a proud and noble cavalry, a train of bronze artillery which was to lay every castle it attacked in ruins, all drawing wages from a well-stocked treasury ... Although the men at arms themselves would have denied it, the wars of the knights were over. 99

It was never easy to keep to the high ideals of chivalry in the real world. Sometimes, in the heat of battle, knights ignored the code completely and behaved like the savagest Dark Age warriors. This was hardly surprising. War is always foul, and men have always been warped by it. Perhaps it is more surprising that *any* knights tried to keep to a chivalrous code of honour.

So warfare in the Age of Chivalry was a dangerous business. But the dangers of death or wounding were smaller than you might think. For one thing, the knights' bodies were well-protected, either by chainmail (see page 6), or, after about 1300, by plate armour. One

*Left:* By the end of the Age of Chivalry, armour for horse and man was often spectacular. This suit was made in Landshut, Germany, between 1475 and 1485.

*Above:* Archers (*left*) could drive charging horses by firing on them from great distances. Pikemen (*right*) with their sharp pikes formed a fearsome barrier to a cavalry charge.

*Above:* Two more men who did not belong to the true Age of Chivalry with its high ideals: the gunner (*left*) and the paid mercenary soldier (*right*).

poet called the knight 'a terrible worm in an iron cocoon'! For another thing, full-scale battles were quite rare. Skirmishes and sieges were far more common. And when commanders *did* decide to risk their expensive knights in a battle, the numbers of casualties could still be low. At the important battle of Bouvines (1214) between France and England, the beaten English lost only 170 knights. It was much more worthwhile to capture and ransom a knight than to kill him outright.

## The show must go on

By 1500 the wars of the knights were over. In peacetime too, the 'nobles of the sword' were losing their powers and privileges. Kings were using more and more 'nobles of the robe' – men of lesser birth but greater learning – to help them to govern their kingdoms. A new ruling class was coming into being, made up of peaceable gentlemen rather than military knights. And gradually the code of chivalry gave way to the less warlike code of 'gentlemanly conduct'. But in spite of all this, the pomp and show of chivalry didn't come to an end. In fact, as the old aristocrats became less important, they grew keener than ever on complicated armour and lavish tourneys, on heraldry and orders of knighthood. They seemed desperate to prove that they really were the grandest people around.

It is hard to say exactly when the Age of Chivalry started or finished. It is easier to see how its *ideals* affected European men and women, in times of war and in times of peace. Ideals are good things to have, even if you can't live up to them all the time. If every medieval knight had stuck to the code of chivalry, Europe would have been a better, safer, fairer place to live in. The knights were only human though. They didn't always practice what they preached. But even so, the code helped to turn brutal Dark Age warriors into more civilized human beings. That was something for everyone to be thankful for. □

1   Why do you think the war poster showed a knight and dragon, and not 20th-century soldiers? Discuss how men might have felt when they saw it. Do you think it is a good poster? – say why or why not.

2   Design a poster of your own, showing what *you* think were the best features of the Age of Chivalry. Take your information from any part of this book.

*Left:* In the Spanish story of Don Quixote by Miguel de Cervantes (1605), the hero was determined to live in a chivalrous way. The book pokes fun at the romances of the Age of Chivalry.

*Below:* A chivalrous knight slays a dangerous dragon. But this poster comes from the 20th century, not from the Age of Chivalry. It urged the men of Britain to volunteer to fight against Germany in World War I (1914–1918).

BRITAIN · NEEDS
YOU · AT · ONCE

# Index

Illustration references are shown in heavy type

**Oxford University Press, Walton St, Oxford OX2 6DP**

Oxford New York Toronto
Delhi Bombay Calcutta Madras Karachi
Petaling Jaya Singapore Hong Kong Tokyo
Nairobi Dar es Salaam Cape Town
Melbourne Auckland

*and associated companies in*

Berlin Ibadan

Oxford is a trademark of Oxford University Press

© **Oxford University Press 1988**

ISBN 0 19 913307 7 (limp, non-net)
ISBN 0 19 913346 8 (cased, net)

Typesetting by MS Filmsetting Ltd, Frome, Somerset
Printed in Hong Kong

**Acknowledgements**

The publishers would like to thank the following for permission to reproduce photographs:
Bibliothèque Nationale, Paris pp4–5, 13 (both), 16, 19 (bottom), 20 (bottom), 23; Bodleian Library, Oxford pp5 (bottom left and right), 7, 11 (both), 14 (both), 17, 18, 24 (bottom), 25 (bottom); British Library, London pp5 (top), 10 (both), 12 (top, reproduced by kind permission of the Duke of Buccleuch), 15, 27 (right), 28 (top), 29 (top and bottom left); the College of Arms p22 (top); English Heritage p9; Giraudon p25 (top); Heidelburg Universitätsbibliothek pp12 (bottom), 19 (top), 20 (top); Michael Holford p8–9; Kunstindustri Museet, Oslo p4; the Order of St John p28 (bottom); the Pierpoint Morgan Library, New York p8; Rex Features p29 (right); Stiftsbibliothek, St Gallen, Switzerland p6; Victoria and Albert Museum, London p27 (left); the Wallace Collection, London p30.

Cover illustration: a fourteenth century tournament (photo – Ikon).

**Illustrated by Richard Hook, Brian Walker and John Ireland**
Dedicated to Andrew, Ian and Andrew